Introduction to the

The Photos App

4th Edition

MacOS Catalina

© iTandCoffee 2020

Special Sales and Supply Queries

For any information about buying this title in bulk quantities, or for supply of this title for educational or fund-raising purposes, contact iTandCoffee on **1300 885 420** or email **enquiry@itandcoffee.com.au**.

iTandCoffee classes and private appointments

For queries about classes and private appointments with iTandCoffee, call **1300 885 420** or email **enquiry@itandcoffee.com.au**.

iTandCoffee operates in and around Camberwell, in Melbourne, Australia.

iTandCoffee
Relax, we'll help you get iT

Introducing iTandCoffee ...

iTandCoffee is a Melbourne-based business that was founded in 2012, by IT professional Lynette Coulston.

Lynette and the staff at iTandCoffee have a passion for helping others - especially women of all ages - to enter and navigate the new, and often daunting, world of technology and to utilise technology to make life easier, not harder!

At iTandCoffee, **patience is our virtue.**

You'll find a welcoming smile, a relaxed cup of tea or coffee, and a genuine enthusiasm for helping you to gain the confidence to use and enjoy your technology.

With personalised appointments and small, friendly classes – either in our bright, comfortable, cafe-style space or at your place - we offer a brand of technology support and education that is so hard to find.

At iTandCoffee, you won't find young 'techies' who speak in a foreign language and move at a pace that leaves you floundering and 'bamboozled'!

Our focus is on helping you to use your technology in a way that enhances your personal and/or professional life – to feel more informed, organised, connected and entertained!

Call on iTandCoffee for help with all sorts of technology – Apple, Windows, Android, iCloud, Evernote, OneDrive, Office 365, Dropbox, all sorts of other Apps, getting you set up on the internet, setting up a printer, and so much more.

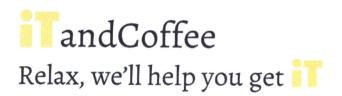

iTandCoffee
Relax, we'll help you get iT

If you are in small business, iTandCoffee has can help in so many ways – with amazing affordable solutions for your business information needs and marketing.

Here are just some of the topics covered in our regular classes at iTandCoffee:

- Introduction to the iPad and iPhone
- Bring your Busy Life under Control using your technology.
- Getting to know your Mac and The Photos app on the Mac
- Understanding and using iCloud
- An Organised Life with Evernote
- Taking and Managing photos on the iPhone and iPad
- Travel with your iPad, iPhone and other technology.
- Keeping kids safe on the iPad, iPhone and iPod Touch.
- Staying Safe Online
- Making the most of your personal technology in your business

The iTandCoffee website (itandcoffee.com.au) offers a wide variety of resources for those brave enough to venture online to learn more: handy hints for iPad, iPhone and Mac; videos and slideshows of iTandCoffee classes; guides on a range of topics; a blog covering all sorts of topical events.

We also produce a regular Handy Hint newsletter full of information that is of interest to our clients and subscribers.

Hopefully, that gives you a bit of a picture of iTandCoffee and what we are about. Please don't hesitate to iTandCoffee on 1300 885 420 to discuss our services or to make a booking.

We hope you enjoy this guide and find its contents informative and useful. Please feel free to offer feedback at feedback@itandcoffee.com.au.

Regards,

Lynette Couston (iTandCoffee Owner)

Introduction to the Mac
The Photos App

TABLE OF CONTENTS

Introduction to the Mac

The Photos App

TABLE OF CONTENTS (cont.)

Introduction to the Mac

The Photos App

TABLE OF CONTENTS (cont.)

Introduction to the Mac
The Photos App
TABLE OF CONTENTS (cont.)

Introduction to the Mac

The Photos App

TABLE OF CONTENTS (cont.)

Introduction

The **Photos** app on your Mac provides a place to manage all your Photos and videos – your 'library' of photos (and videos.)

By importing all photos and videos using the **Photos** app (into your **Photos Library**), it is then possible to view, organise and share them in multiple ways.

Photos (and videos) can be viewed on a **timeline,** allowing a 'drill-down' to a photo or set of photos based on when the photo was taken – starting first with **Years**, then **Months** within a Year, and then **Days** within the month. We'll look at this 'timeline' view shortly.

Photos and videos can also be viewed as 'Memories', by places, people and other 'albums', presented in slide shows, shared with others via iCloud, and more.

Your other Mac applications can use your photos/videos and albums that are stored in your **Photos** library - for example, when inserting a photo in your email, the search screen allows you to browse **Photos** for the image you wish to include.

It is important to understand that, while a particular photo may appear under more than one 'album' or in more than one of the library areas, that photo exists only once in the library.

When you place a photo into an album, **you are not moving it or copying it**. We'll talk about this in more detail throughout this guide.

A Guided Tour of Photos

Let's look first at the various areas of the Photos App. For those of you who used Photos under MacOS Sierra or earlier, you will notice that there are quite a few changes in the subsequent versions of Photos.

The Sidebar

Let's look first at the Sidebar on the left.

In Sierra and earlier, the sidebar was something that could be turned on and off (from the View menu). Since High Sierra, it has been a permanent fixture.

The arrangement of options in this sidebar also changed in High Sierra. The main sections are now Library, Shared (depending on your iCloud settings), Albums, and Projects. This has not changed in Mojave and Catalina.

Let's look at the different sections shown in the Sidebar.

Before we do, it is important to note that the content of each section in the sidebar can be hidden.

If you are only seeing the name of any section and not its contents, hover the mouse over the section name and click the word **Show**. In the same way, you can **Hide** the contents of each section.

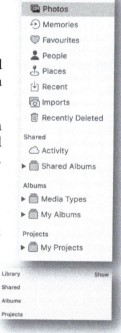

A Guided Tour of Photos

Library

The top section of the sidebar is the **Library,** which provides several options for viewing your photos, each of which we will cover in more detail in subsequent pages.

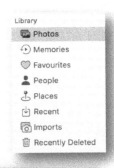

Photos   View your whole photo library as timeline, based on 'Date Taken'.
Options along the top allow you to choose different ways to view this full collection of photos:

Years	Months	Days	All Photos

Years	View your photos grouped by Year
Months	View your photos grouped by Month
Day	View your photos grouped by Day
All Photos	View your timeline of photos ungrouped

Memories   The Photos app will automatically create 'curated collections' of your photos, to help you re-discover forgotten memories buried in your photos. Visit this option regularly to see your new 'Memories'.

Favourites   View those photos you have marked as your 'Favourites'. (This option used to appear under the Albums section in the Sierra version of Photos.)

People   The Photos app helps you identify and group photos of people, so that you can view collections of photos for the various people in your life. (This option used to appear under the Albums section in the Sierra version of Photos.)

Places   View your photos on a map, based on the location that was recorded against the photo when it was taken. (This option used to appear under the Albums section in the Sierra version of Photos.)

Zoom in and out on this map to 'split out' your photos by their location. It is a great way of seeing all the places you have been!

Recents   Your photos listed in the order in which they appeared on this Mac (instead of their 'date taken' order). So, if you just saved

A Guided Tour of Photos

a photo to your Mac from, say, an email, it will appear as the last photo – even it that photo was taken a while ago.

Imports   This was a handy new feature of Photos in MacOS High Sierra. Imports allows you to view your photos according to when they were imported. (The Last Import option used to appear under the Albums section in the Sierra version of Photos.)

Recently Deleted

Deleted photos are moved to this area and retained for around 30 days, after which they are deleted. (This option used to appear under the Albums section in the Sierra version of Photos.)

Shared

The next main section of the sidebar is the **Shared** section

The shared section includes the photos and Albums found in your iCloud Shared Albums area. This section will only appear if you have chosen to enable **Shared**. This is covered more fully a bit later.

Albums

The third section of the sidebar is the **Albums** section

(This section of the sidebar underwent a substantial rearrangement in MacOS High Sierra when compared to Sierra.)

As already touched on above, some of the albums that previously 'lived' in this section were moved up under the 'Library' section (Favourites, People, Places, Imports, Recently Deleted) in the transition from Sierra to later versions.

The other content of Albums has now been separated into two main sub-sections – **Media Types** and **My Albums**.

A Guided Tour of Photos

Media Types groups your photos according to their type – videos, selfies, live photos, etc. Photos will automatically appear in these albums based on their format/type.

The **My Albums** sub-section contains the Folders and Albums that you create, something that we cover in more detail later.

Projects

The final section of the sidebar is the **Projects** section, listing any projects you have created using your photos – photo books, calendars, card, slideshows, prints.

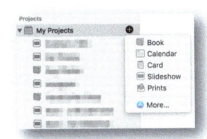

Toolbar options

In most views of the Photos app, you will notice a set of symbols at the top right. Let's look at the meaning of these symbols – we'll then cover these things in more detail later.

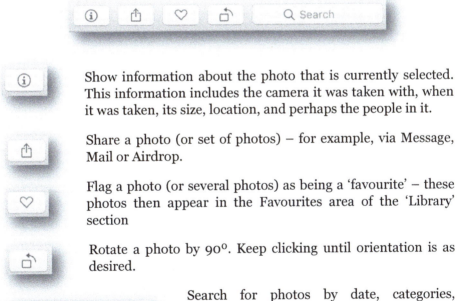

Show information about the photo that is currently selected. This information includes the camera it was taken with, when it was taken, its size, location, and perhaps the people in it.

Share a photo (or set of photos) – for example, via Message, Mail or Airdrop.

Flag a photo (or several photos) as being a 'favourite' – these photos then appear in the Favourites area of the 'Library' section

Rotate a photo by 90°. Keep clicking until orientation is as desired.

Search for photos by date, categories, keywords, people, and more. As an example, type 'dog' in this search field to find all photos with a dog.

A Guided Tour of Photos

Showing

In many views of thumbnails of your photos – Albums, All Photos, Recents and various other place, you will see the **Showing** option on the top right-hand side, below the Search bar..

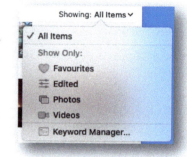

This option allows you to choose to filter the photos you are viewing, to only see Favourites, or only Edited photos, only Photos, or only Videos.

Viewing your Photo Library as Days, Months, Years

All of our photos have a 'date taken' associated with them, recorded by the camera or smartphone/tablet when the photo was taken. (For a camera, this means that the date must have been correctly set at that point in time.)

Information like 'date-taken' is known as the **metadata** associated with your photos. Location information can also be recorded as part of your photo's metadata, depending on the device used to take the photo.

The Photos app uses the 'date taken' and 'location' information to show your photos on a timeline, allowing you to view all the photos taken by **Year**, then **Month**, then by individual **Days** or sets of days and places. You can also view **All Photos** in date order.

(Note. In Catalina, this 'Years, Months, Days, All Photos' naming/grouping of the photos in this area replaced the previous 'Photos, Moments, Collections, Years' naming/grouping that has applied for the past few macOS versions).

| Years | Months | Days | All Photos |

Clicking the **Photos** option in the sidebar (in the **Library** section) provides the ability to view this timeline of photos grouped according to these groupings.

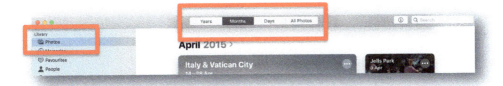

Viewing your Photo Library as Moments, Collection, Years

The four options are shown along the top when the Photos option is selected from the Library section in the Sidebar. Let's look now at these four ways of viewing your photos timeline.

Years

The **Years** view shows large 'thumbnails' of each the years that are represented by your collection of photos, according to each photo's 'date taken'.

(Note. We'll cover later how you can adjust this 'date taken' so that photos with incorrect dates – eg. scanned old photos – appear in the correct place on this timeline.)

Double-click on any of these thumbnails to view the photos represented by that year, grouped by month.

Months

Months view provides a summary of photos, listed in Month order – with large thumbnails to represent collections of photos within each month.

Double-click on any of these large thumbnails to ⬤ view the associated photos, or click the symbol at top right of the thumbnail.

Viewing your Photo Library as Moments, Collection, Years

You will see the options:

- **Play** to view a slideshow (with music) of the set of photos or

- **Show Map** to view the set of photos on a map. (Note. The Show Map option will only appear if the photos represented by the thumbnail have location information recorded against them.)

To see all the photos associated with the month and surrounding months, click the **All Photos** option when you have the applicable month in view.

Days

The **Days** view provides individual photos, or thumbnails representing the photos taken on a particular date or set of dates.

Double-click on any **thumbnail*** of a photo in your **Days** view to view that individual photo.

To see all the photos associated with that day and surrounding days, click the **All Photos** option when you have the applicable date in view.

If you see a number in an oval at the bottom right of a thumbnail (as shown  right), this means there are a number of further photos associated that date. Click the number to view those photos.

Right-click (or two-finger click) any photo's thumbnail to see a menu of options that apply to the selected photo (see right).

Viewing your Photo Library as Moments, Collection, Years

In the **Days** view, you will also see a 'zoom' slider in the top bar, towards the left (near the 'traffic lights').

This slider allows the size of the thumbnails to be enlarged and reduced to suit your requirements – handy when you are searching for a photo or comparing similar photos.

All Photos

The **All Photos** view allows for the viewing of all photos by 'date taken'.

If you have a Month or Day in view when you click the All Photos option, the set of photos you see first in All Photos relate to that Month/Day.

Use the slider at the top left to adjust the size of the thumbnails you see.

As shown here, the thumbnails can be made very small, to allow you to scan for a point in time and photo.

Double-click on any thumbnail to view the photo, then use your arrow keys to move through the photos before and after that photo.

Other options for viewing your Library

Favourites

Favourites shows any photos you've marked as being favourites –

- by clicking the heart icon at the top when viewing the individual photo, or
- by clicking the heart in the bottom left corner of the thumnail as you hover over the applicable thumbnail.

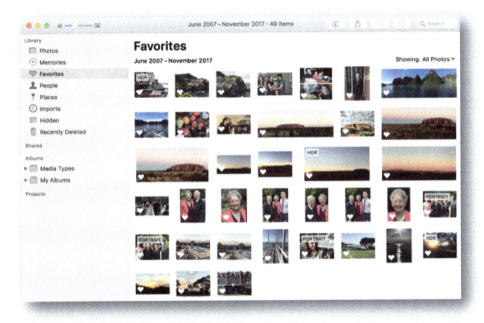

To remove a favourite, just click on it (or on several) and click the heart symbol in the toolbar at top right. The 'un-favourited' photos will disappear from the Favourites view.

If you are not using iCloud Photos (covered towards the end of this guide), **Favourites** you have chosen on your iPad or iPhone are separate to those on your Mac. This means that, even if you have 'hearted' a photo on you iPhone, it won't automatically appear in Favourites on your Mac (or your iPad, for that matter).

(iCloud Photos users will find that syncing of Favourites *DOES* occur between devices.)

Other options for viewing your Library

People

This special album splits photos into groupings according to facial recognition.

Those people you deem your 'favourites' can be shown at the top, and you can 'merge' sets of photos that the Photos app has matched, to build up comprehensive set of photos of each person.

We'll cover this more fully a bit later in this guide.

Places

The Places view of your photos Library shows your photos according to the location at which they were taken – for those photos that have location information stored in their metadata. Along the top of this view, you will see three options – **Map**, **Satellite** and **Grid** – providing different ways of viewing the groupings of your photos by 'place'.

In **Map** view, thumbnails of photos are shown on a map, where each thumbnail shows the number of photos taken at each location. Double-click on any of these thumbnails to view those photos.

Zoom in and out on this map to 'split out' your photos by their location.

Use the – and + at the bottom right of the screen to zoom.

Click and hold on the circle that surrounds the 3D button to rotate the map itself.

Other options for viewing your Library

Satellite view is very similar to **Map** view – except that it shows your photos on a satellite image, on which you can then zoom in to see birds-eye views of where your photos were taken.

This is an amazing feature, allowing you to revisit the places where your photos were taken – and even use the 3D feature, in conjunction with the + and – (bottom right) zoom and see the location in 3D.

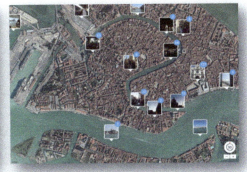

Other options for viewing your Library

Grid view shows the photos of places as thumbnails, grouped by location.

View an individual photo by double-clicking on it. Or Click on the > next to the location to view the location's photos in **Explore View**

Recent

The **Recent** option is new in macOS Catalina and provides the ability to view your photos according to date they 'arrived on' the Mac.

This means that the order you see here may be different to that you see in the **Photos** views described earlier, since a photo taken several years ago but just saved to Photos will appear as the last photo.

To see any photo from the **Recent** view in its 'date' order (and with other photos taken on the same or adjacent dates), right click on the photo in **Recent** and choose **Show in All Photos**

Imports

The Imports view in Library shows the photos according to the date they were imported to your Mac from a Camera, SD Card, iPhone or iPad, or any another import method – see later in this guide for methods of importing photos you your Photos library.

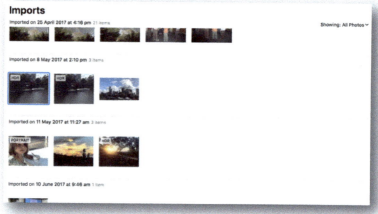

Other options for viewing your Library

My Photo Stream

Depending on your Photos app's **Settings**, you may see the **My Photo Stream** album in your Albums list. (Note. My Photos Stream is being phased out and is not available for newer iCloud accounts.)

This album contains the photos that have been 'streamed' to your device via iCloud. Refer later in this document for more information about My Photo Stream.

(If iCloud Photos is turned On, you will not see the My Photo Stream album – even if the feature is enabled.)

Hidden

The **Hidden** album includes any photos you have chosen to keep hidden from the casual observer!

Photos lets you choose whether the **Hidden** album appears under the Library section. It can remain out of sight if you desire.

Go to the **View** menu in the top menu bar and choose **Hide Hidden Photo Album** to hide it or **Show Hidden Photo Album** to include it under Library

Photos can be hidden from other Library views by right-clicking (or two-finger-clicking) on any photo (or a set of photos) and choosing **Hide 1 Photo** or **Hide *n* Photos** (where '*n*' is the number of photos you have selected).

Refer later for instructions on how to select multiple images.

Recently Deleted

Just as it sounds, the Recently Deleted album holds photos you have decided to 'trash'.

The Photos App retains deleted photos and videos for about 30 days (sometimes up to 40 days), in case you make a mistake and need to retrieve them.

Other options for viewing your Library

Photos in this album show the days remaining before permanent deletion.

To permanently delete the photos from this album (and thereby free up their allocated storage), just choose **Delete All** (which will be at top right) when viewing this Album.

Alternatively, if you find you have deleted a photo or video in error, just select **Recently Deleted**, select the applicable photo/s (by clicking on it/them), and choose **Recover** (at top right).

Viewing individual photos/videos

Getting to a single photo/video

From any view that shows 'thumbnails' of your photos, **double-click** on any image's thumbnail to view the individual photo.

Alternatively, if an item is already selected (i.e. it has a blue border around it), press the space bar to view that item. (Pressing the space bar again will also bring you back to the thumbnail view.)

Then, use the right and left arrow keys on your keyboard to move to the next or previous photo.

Alternatively, you can swipe left or right using your apple mouse or trackpad.

Zoom in and out when viewing the photo using the slider at top left of the screen.

Viewing individual photos/videos

Returning to previous 'view'

Use the < symbol at top left to go 'back up' to the previous level (eg. back to the applicable Thumbnail view).

Double-clicking on the individual photo that you are viewing will have the same effect as clicking the < symbol.

View in Full Screen

To view your photo or video in full-screen mode, click the green traffic light.

Press Esc to on your keyboard to exit full-screen mode.

Play a video

If the item is a video, you will see a bar of symbols when you bring the mouse pointer over the image on the screen.

- **To play a video:** Click the 'Play' symbol ▶

- **To stop a video:** Click the double bars ‖

Explore view

The **Explore** view allows you to look at where a photo was taken on a map, to view other 'nearby photos', and to see other 'related' photos.

The look of this 'view' is very similar to the 'Memories' view, described in the next section.

To see the *Explore* view, **scroll up** while viewing an individual photo.

Viewing individual photos/videos

Your toolbar of options

When you are viewing an individual photo or video, you will see some options at the top right. The set of option available is as follows:

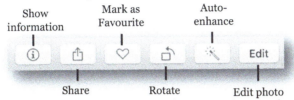

We will look at these options throughout the upcoming sections of this guide, but for now let's just look at the 'Heart' option.

'Heart' your favourites

You may have noticed that the bar of options that is visible when viewing individual photos includes the ♡ option.

The ♡ option allows you to specify certain photos as your 'Favourites'.

Click on this heart to 'Favourite' a photo that you are currently viewing. The photo will then automatically appear in the **Favourites** album.

Any photo that has been set as a 'Favourite' will show a shaded heart. Just click the heart again to remove the photo from your Favourites.

See any photo with other photos from that same day

This is something I find very handy, especially when checking for duplicated photos or wanting to check what other similar photos exist for a photo I have put in an album or that appears in my **All Photos** view.

If you are viewing a photo in a view other than Days/All Photos (either as a full thumbnail or in individual photo view), right-click (or two-finger-click) on it and choose **Show in All Photos**

This will take you straight to the **All Photos** view, with the selected photo highlighted with a blue border, and showing all the other photos taken on and around the same date.

Memories -
Re-visit your past through photos

The Memories option was introduced to the Photos app by Mac OS Sierra and iOS 10, late in 2016.

Here is how Apple describes this feature:

"Rediscover favourite and forgotten moments from deep in your photo library. Memories automatically creates curated collections of your most meaningful photos and videos."

The contents of the **Memories** area will be chosen for you automatically by the Photos app, from (supposedly) the best photos in the library (although I'm not convinced this is always true!).

You will see 'Memories' like those shown in the screen shot on the right. Just double-click on a particular Memory you wish to view

At the top is a movie/slideshow of the photos in the 'Memory'. A summary of the photos in the 'Memory' is shown below that, with the option to **Show All** (or **Show More**)- which shows all the photos in that memory.

Thumbnails of the 'people' appearing in the 'Memory' are shown, as is a map with the location of the Memory's photos and other 'related Memories'.

Memories -
Re-visit your past through photos

If you like the Memory, you can choose to keep it – by adding it to your Favourites. Choose **Add to Favourite Memories**.

Add to Favorite Memories

Delete Memory

If you don't like a particular Memory, just delete it by choosing **Delete Memory** – to stop it appearing again.

These options are available at the bottom of the **Memory** view, when viewing an individual Memory.

I must say that I have not made much use of this feature on the Mac yet, but do visit it on my iPad and iPhone, as those devices play the Memory as a lovely pre-made movie/slideshow.

For further details on the Memory feature, check out the Apple Support article https://support.apple.com/en-au/HT207023.

Introducing Albums

As mentioned earlier, the Photos app allows for the organising of photos (and videos) by arranging them into **Albums**, or for viewing of photos in standard Albums that Apple has provided for you.

Albums that you create can then be grouped into 'Folders' – providing a great way of being able to find the photos you are looking for.

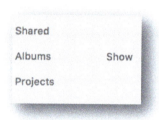

If you don't see anything listed in the Albums area of your sidebar, hover the mouse pointer over the word **Albums** so that the word **Show** appears on the right.

Click this **Show** option to reveal the list of albums. (The same action then allows you to 'hide' the list of Albums again.)

As described earlier, the **Albums** section now includes two major sub-sections – **Media Types** and **My Albums**

Media Types contains albums that group photos according to their type. This occurs automatically, based on each photo's metadata.

The Media Types albums cannot be deleted and will only appear if you have any photos of the type represented by that album.

Lets look first at these **Media Type** albums that are provided by Apple.

We'll look at the **My Albums** section when we talk later about how to organise your photos.

Albums - Media Types

To view the full set of **Media Types** albums, click on the ▶ that is on its left – this will expand the list of albums under this area.

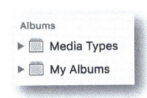

As already mentioned, the set of albums you see listed under **Media Types** will depend on the photos that are in your Library. This means that you may not see the full set of albums shown on the right.

Here are the possible albums that will appear:

Videos

As you can probably guess, the Videos album shows all the videos that are in your Photos Library.

Selfies

This album shows any photos in the library that were taken with the front camera of your iPad or iPhone (or the Facetime camera on your Mac).

Screenshots

This album shows any 'screen shots' taken on your iPad or iPhone.

Screen shots on your iPad and iPhone are pictures taken by pressing the sleep switch and home button simultaneously on the iPad or iPhone. (On the iPhone X series and new iPad Pro's, the combination of buttons is different – it is the 'Sleep' and 'Volume Up' combination that takes a screen shot).

This takes a photo of whatever is currently showing on the device's screen and stores this photo in your Photos app on that device, in the Camera Roll (or All Photos if iCloud Photos is enabled).

Live Photos, Panoramas, Slo-Mo, Time Lapse and Bursts, Portrait, Animated

These albums show any photos that you took with your iPad/iPhone and using the corresponding feature from that device.

Selecting Photos

Before we get into talking about creating your own albums, we need to cover a couple of other things relating to managing your photos – selecting photos and deleting photos.

Quite often, you will have the need to select more than one photo – for example, to select a set of photos to add to an album, to delete, to put in a slideshow, to share and more. There are several ways to select photos:

Select a single photo

Just click on a thumbnail or double-click to open that photo.

Select multiple random photos:

Multiple random photos can be selected (and unselected) in full thumbnail view by **holding down the Command Key** as you click on each item in the view.

Select inclusive range of photos:

An inclusive range of photos can be selected by clicking the first photo in the range and then, as you click the last photo in the range, **holding down the Shift key**.

Select all photos:

Click any image in the thumbnail view and then choose **Command-A** (select all) to select all in that view.

Unselect selected photos:

If you have selected multiple photos, you can then **unselect** certain of these photos by **holding down the Command Key** as you click the photo/s.

Selected photos are indicated with a blue border.

Refer to this page whenever we talk about selecting photos throughout this guide.

Deleting photos

Understanding 'Delete' vs 'Remove'

Photos can be **Deleted** a few different ways.

But before we discuss these methods, we need to first look at the difference between 'Removing' a photo from an Album and 'Deleting' a photo.

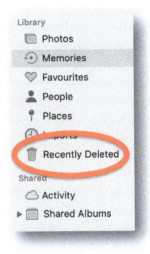

Always make sure you check the message that appears when you are deleting, to confirm if you are actually 'deleting' or 'removing'. What do I mean by this?

If you are looking in one of the Library areas or in a Media Types album, and you choose to Delete any of these photos, you will be **deleting** the photos from the Photos Library.

They will go into the **Recently Deleted** album and be permanently deleted after 30 days (approx.).

If you are looking at a set of photos that are in a My Albums album, one that you have created (we'll look at creating your own albums shortly), you will just be 'removing' the photo/s from that Album, but leaving them in the Photos library and in any other Album that you have added them to. The same applies to photos in a **Memory.**

(That is, unless you specifically choose the 'Delete' option described by the second bullet point below, where you right-click on photo/s and choose **Delete** instead of **Remove**.)

If you are going through a process of deleting unwanted photos, it is best to be viewing one of the **Library** or **Media Types** views, not viewing them in an Album you created yourself.

Ways to Delete

1. If you are viewing an individual photo in one of the Library views or in Media Types, select the **delete** key on the keyboard, then confirm by selecting the **Delete** button from the message that appears.

Deleting Photos

2. Right-click (or two-finger-click) on the selected photo/s (refer earlier for methods of selecting multiple photos) and choose the **Delete** option from the list of options that appear. You will see the same confirmation message that appeared in option 1 – select **Delete** to confirm

3. If you want to delete without having to confirm, select one or more photos (refer earlier) and choose ⌘–**delete (Command-Delete)** on the keyboard.

Removing photos from your own Albums

When you are viewing photos in an album that you have created, just select the Delete key on the keyboard to remove the photo from the album.

The photo will **not** be removed from any other Albums or from the Library.

If you truly want to delete a photo that appears in one of your own albums – and delete it completely from the library – use options 2 or 3 described in *Ways to Delete* above.

Where do Deleted photos go?

As mentioned earlier, deleted photos and videos will be moved to the **Recently Deleted** album.

If a photo was incorrectly deleted, go to the **Recently Deleted** album, select the photo or photos, and choose **Recover** (top right).

Photos 'removed' from a personal album or Memory will still be available in the Photos library and can be re-added to the album/Memory if required.

Deleting Photos

Some hidden space gobblers to delete

If you have a newer iPhone or iPad – one that is capable of taking 'Bursts' (rapid-fire photos taken by holding down the white dot, instead of just tapping that dot), you may find yourself with quite a few 'bursts' of several photos, instead of just the single photo that you want.

Visit the **Bursts** album under **Media Types** to find and eradicate these extra photos.

In the example shown here, I can see that there are several sets of 'bursts' in my **Bursts** album.

What I really want to do is choose the best of each set of photos and delete the rest. To do this, double-click to view one of the 'bursts'. At top left of the photo is **Make a Selection**. Click this to view the full set of photos in the burst.

Along the bottom shows a ribbon of the photos in the burst.

Click each photo in this ribbon in turn, and choose to 'tick' or 'untick' it – to show that you do or don't want to keep that photo.

Deleting Photos

Once you have chosen which photos you want to keep from the burst, choose **Done** at top right.

If you have ticked a selection of the burst's photos (one or more), you will be asked what to do with those that you didn't select.

Usually, you will want to click **Keep Only Selection**, so that the unselected photos are moved to the Recently Deleted album (and eventually deleted).

A Handy Tip if you make a mistake when deleting

Don't forget that, in most cases, you can **Undo your last action** – for example, restore incorrectly deleted photos – by simultaneously pressing the two keys.

⌘-Z (Command-z)

The Edit menu provides the same '**Undo**' option, in case you forget this keyboard combination. It even shows you exactly what the ⌘-Z combination will 'Undo'.

Also available in the Edit menu is the **Redo** option, should you decide that you need to reverse the 'Undo'.

The exception to this is if you Delete your photos from the Recently Deleted album. This **cannot** be undone.

Organising your Photos - Find your People

The **People** album under **Library** offers a great way of viewing all the photos of a particular person, using facial recognition to discover and group photos.

The first time you visit the People album in MacOS High Sierra, your Photos app will show a set of thumbnails that represent sets of photos that have been determined as showing the same person. Double-click on any of these thumbnails to view the set of photos that have been found for that person.

Name your people

By hovering the mouse pointer over a photo's thumbnail, you will see  appear at the bottom left of the thumbnail.

Click here to assign a name to the person.

A list of suggested contacts will appear below – just click on the relevant person, or (if they are not a Contact) keep typing the name and choose enter/return to complete.

At that point, you may see another screen appear, asking for confirmation of some other faces that are deemed to be close matches to the person in the thumbnail that you just named.

Organising your Photos -
Find your People

Select (by clicking circle at bottom right of each thumbnail to tick/un-tick) those thumbnails that are the same person as that you named, and then choose **Done**.

This will collate even more photos of that same person.

If you name the person in the thumbnail and it is found that there is already a named thumbnail for that same person, the below screen will appear, asking for confirmation that the two thumbnails represent the same person.

If they do, select **Yes**, which will merge the two sets of photos into one.

Otherwise, select **Cancel**

Remove unwanted people

You will probably see the faces of people you barely know or are not really important to you.

These faces can be removed from the People album.

Right-click (or two-finger-click) on the thumbnail and choose the option **Remove this Person.**

Confirm by selecting **Remove from People Album** when you see the confirmation message below.

Nominate your favourites

Your most important people can be 'hearted' by clicking the small heart at the bottom right of each thumbnail.

This nominates that the person is a 'favourite'.

Favourites then appear at the top of the People screen, as larger thumbnails than the rest.

Organising your Photos - Find your People

Identifying more photos of the same person

For each identified 'Person', double-click the thumbnail on the main People screen to view the 'already-matched' photos of that person, shown as a 'Memories' style screen with lots of ways of viewing photos of the person.

Scroll down that screen to see some additional options at the very bottom.

Click **Confirm Additional Photos** to look for more photos of the same person.

You will then be taken through a series of photos and asked to confirm if each one is (or is not) the applicable person. Click 'Yes' if the photos IS of the person, and 'No' otherwise.

Choose **Done** at top right to finish, or wait until you have exhausted all the possible potential matches.

You will see the total number of additional photos that you just added for that person.

Confirming just a few additional matches can add a substantial number of photos to the set collated for that person.

Merge People

If you see more than one thumbnail for the same person, the sets of photos represented by these thumbnails can be merged.

Select the applicable thumbnails (using the *command* key as you click each), then right-click (or two-finger-click) on one of them to see this list of options.

Choose **Merge n People** (where n is the number of thumbnails you selected) to combine. You will see the below confirmation message.

Select **Yes** to complete the merging process.

Organising your Photos - Find your People

Identifying people while viewing photos

There is another way of updating your People album and adding to the photos for each of your people.

While you are viewing individual photos, you can turn on a feature that shows the name of each identified person in the photo and shows **unnamed** for anyone who hasn't been identified yet.

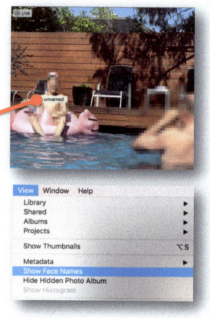

Go to the **View** menu at the top and choose **Show Face Names.**

Click on **unnamed** under any faces that are not yet identified, and type in the name of the person.

If someone is incorrectly identified, type in their correct identity in the box under their face.

Turn off this feature again by visiting the **View** Menu and choosing **Hide Face Names.**

When the wrong person appears in a People album

Of course, the face recognition technology is not perfect – so you may find that, when you have a look at the set of photos for a person, there are photos of other people included.

It is easy to remove any incorrectly matched photos from a People album.

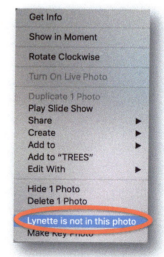

Double-click on the person's thumbnail to view the set of photos of that person.

For any photo or photos that does not belong, right click (or two-finger-click) on the photo/s and choose *Person-name* **is not in this photo**

Organising your Photos - Find your People

Make Key Photos

To change the photo that is used as the 'thumbnail' for a person in the screen showing your collection of People, find the photo that you prefer, right-click on it (or two-finger click, if applicable) and choose **Make Key Photo**.

Organising your Photos - Creating an Album

Many of us end up with a huge number of photos on our Mac.

While the timeline functionality in the Photos view, and the Memories, People, Places and other features allow us to find the photos we are looking for, most of us want to also organise our photos into our own Albums, albums that contain the photos for a particular occasion, holiday, person, place or other grouping.

Albums offer a great way of showcasing your photos to family and friends, and a great way of organising your images so that you can find them when you need them! A photo can appear in multiple Albums that you create.

Create an album

Before you create an album, it is important to decide if you want to create an 'empty' album (and add photos after its creation), or whether you want to select some photos and then create an album for those photos.

If you want an empty album, just ensure that you don't have any photos selected. If any photos have a blue border around them (indicating they are in the current selection), just click in the white space surrounding the photos to cancel the current selection.

There are then several ways to create a new album.

Option 1: From the menu bar, select
File -> New Album

Option 2: Click on **My Albums** in the sidebar, and you will see a + on the right. Click this + to create a new album.

Option 3: Right-click on **My Albums** (or on any folder that you have already created in My Albums) and choose **New Album**

Organising your Photos - Creating an Album

Option 4: If you have some photos selected, right-click (or two-finger-click) and choose **Add to** (or find the same option in the **Image** menu). You will then see a list of options – click the first option, **New Album**.

Option 5: Click on **My Albums**, and you will see your set of albums on the right-hand side of the screen.

Right-click anywhere in the white space in this area and choose **New Album.**

For each of these options, a new album – called **Untitled Album** - will appear under the **My Albums** section in the sidebar.

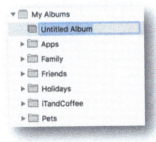

If it is already highlighted in blue (as shown left), simply type in the name for the new album.

If the name is not highlighted, click once to select the album, then again to get into 'edit' mode to change the name.

Or right-click on the un-named album and choose **Rename Album.**

We will also shortly cover how to create **Folders**, which are collections of albums (and, perhaps, folders).

If you already have folders in your My Albums area, it is easy to add an album to that folder.

Just click on the folder and choose the + symbol that appears on the right side.

Organising your Photos - Adding Photos/Videos to an Album

Adding photos to an existing album is very easy – there are several ways to achieve this.

Use Drag and Drop

One way to add photos to an existing album is to simply select one or more photos and drag them across to on top of the name of the Album.

A blue bar will appear across the Album Name to show that it is the one that is selected. If you let go, the selected photos will 'drop into' that album.

Use Add to

As mentioned earlier for creating a new album add to an existing album by, right-clicking (or two-finger-clicking) on any of the selected photos and choose **Add to**.

(This **Add to** option is also available from the **Image** menu.)

From the list shown, choose the album to which the photos should be added.

In the example on the right, I had to hover over the folder 'Friends' to allow me to select one of the albums within that folder.

Organising your Photos - Managing Albums

Renaming an Album

If you want to rename an existing Album, just right-click on it in the Sidebar and choose 'Rename Album', then enter the new name for the Album.

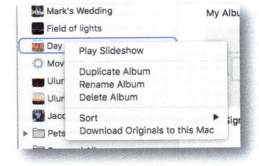

Or, if viewing the albums as 'Thumbnails', just click on the name underneath the thumbnail, and change.

Rearranging Albums

Albums can be listed in the order that you choose. Just click and drag the Album to the required location. A blue line (see right) will show the position where the Album will be moved – just release the mouse or trackpad to 'drop' the Album to that position.

If you are viewing the albums as thumbnails, just click and drag the Album thumbnail to the required position.

The other albums will 'move aside', and you can 'drop' the album in the space that is made.

Organising your Photos - Managing Albums

Deleting Albums

Deleting an Album that you have created will simply remove the Album and its corresponding grouping of photos.

The photos in the album will still exist in the Photos library and in any other Album in which they have been placed.

If you want to delete an Album, just right-click on it in the Sidebar or on its thumbnail and choose '**Delete Album**'

Sorting Photos within an Album

Photos within an album that you create can be sorted manually, or can be sorted automatically by title, or date-taken.

Just right-click on the album name and choose **Sort**. Then choose the desired sort option as shown in the below image.

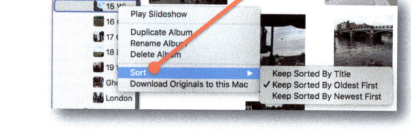

If you would like to manually sort your photos, just ensure that no options are ticked in the Sort option. To 'untick', just click on the option that is ticked.

If none of these 'automatic sort' options are ticked, you will be able to drag photos into the order you require. In this case, photos added to the album will appear at the end of the album's photos, ready to be re-arranged.

Organising your Photos - Managing Albums

Grouping Albums into Folders

Over time, you may find that you end up with a very long list of Albums – and need to be able to group these Albums together, and perhaps 'hide' the albums you are not currently using.

In the Photos app, it is possible to set up a whole structure of folders and sub-folders for storing Albums.

Folders don't store photos, so you can't drag photos into a folder. A folder can only contain albums and other folders.

To create a Folder, simple choose **File->New Folder**.

The new folder will appear under My Albums, with the name **Untitled Folder**. As for albums, this name can then be changed

If you had clicked on an existing folder in your **My Albums** list before choosing the **New Folder** option, then the new folder will be created inside the folder that you had selected.

 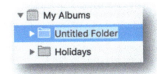

Alternative ways of creating folders

As we saw for Albums, there are a few other ways to create folders.

Choose the + symbol that appears when you click on **My Albums** or any of your already-created folders.

Or right-click on **My Albums** or any existing folder and choose **New Folder**

As with Albums, you can also right-click on the white space around album/folder thumbnails to see the same option.

Organising your Photos - Managing Albums

Populate your folder

Once the folder is created, drag albums or other folders on top of this new folder to move them to that folder.

Any folder containing albums or other folders will show ▶ on the left.

Click this symbol to expand the folder and see its contents.

Click the downward arrow again to 'collapse up' the contents of the folder.

Creating a Folder Structure

To create folders within folders, simply drag one folder on top of the other.

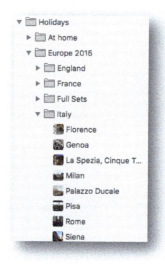

You can create a multi-level folder structure, helping to keep all those albums easy to find.

When using the Sidebar, you can also right-click on any Folder and choose New Folder to create a folder within that folder.

In the example on the right, I can easily find the holiday photos that I took in Italy when we travelled to Europe in 2015.

Renaming Folders

Renaming and re-arranging folders can be done in the same way as described above for Albums.

To rename, just right-click on the folder name and choose **Rename Folder**.

Alternatively, select the folder then click again on the name to get into 'edit' mode to change the name.

Organising your Photos - Managing Albums

Deleting Folders

Right-clicking on the folder name also gives the **Delete Folder** option.

Deleting a folder will simply remove the folder and any folders and albums it contains.

The photos that were in the folders albums will still exist in the photo library.

Rearranging and sorting Folders

Drag folders around to manually re-order.

To automatically sort folders (or folders/albums within folders), right-click on the folder name or on the **My Albums** heading to choose the **Sort** option.

Choose to sort by **By Name**, **By Newest First** or **By Newest First**.

Sharing Photos and Videos

The Photos app allows the sharing of the photos (and videos) from your Photos Library, using email, Messages, iCloud, Facebook and Airdrop. You can also add them to Notes, set an image as your Desktop picture, and more.

You can choose to share an individual photo or video, or several at once (although limits apply in certain cases).

Sharing photos or videos

Choose one or more photos (or videos) using the method described earlier in **Select Photos**

Then click  at top right to uncover your set of 'Share' options.

Click on the required 'Share' option from the list shown.

Depending on what Apps you have on your Mac, you may be able to add additional 'share' apps by clicking on the **More...** option.

Emailing photos

Choose the **Mail** option in share to send one or more photos via email.

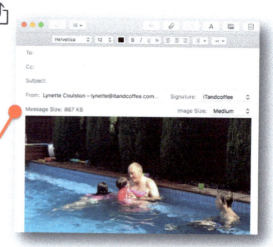

If you send multiple images, just make sure that the email you are creating is not too big to send.

The size of the email is shown in **Message Size.**

If the email with images is over 500KB in size, you will be given the option to send the images as a smaller size.

Sharing Photos and Videos

The file size of the photos that you send can be adjusted using the **Image Size** field. Just click on this to see the various sizes that you can send, and to choose that which will apply to the current email. The **Message Size** will adjust when you change the **Image Size**.

This image size setting will then be 'remembered' for the next email that you send.

This means that, if you adjust the size to Medium when sending a set of photos via email today, then the next time you create an email with photos, they will be automatically sized as Medium.

This can then be changed if you require a different sizing next time around – and will again be 'remembered'.

Sharing Photos with others via iCloud

A set of photos can also be shared using your iCloud, by setting up **Shared Albums.**

We will cover this in more detail later in this guide, as it gets us into the more complex territory that is iCloud!

Sharing photos using Airdrop

If you are looking to share photos or videos with another Apple user who is nearby (i.e. a matter of metres away), *Airdrop* allows for such sharing with other Apple devices (Mac, iPad and iPhone) without requiring internet access – using Bluetooth instead.

This can be very handy for a sharing a large group of photos or videos, avoiding size limits that may apply to email or messages and other sharing that requires internet access.

Viewing your photos as a Slideshow

The **Slideshow** option allows your Photos app to automatically cycle through an album or set of photos, showing your images/videos.

You can have fancy 'transitions' and can even play your show with music – your own music, if you so desire.

The Slideshow option is available when you are viewing thumbnails of photos in an Album, and in certain other views. Look for the word Slideshow, or (in certain places) for the 'play' symbol ▶.

Clicking either of these will result in some options for presenting your slideshow – the 'theme' and the 'music'.

The **Theme** will determine the 'style' of the slideshow – try out each theme to work out which one suits. A preview of the theme (and the default music that will play with it) will show in the small window above the theme names.

If you have any music in your iTunes library, you may be able to choose a single track to play with your Slideshow (instead of the default music).

Just choose the **Music** option at the top to see the music that you can choose from. Only

Viewing your photos as a Slideshow

music that is stored on your Mac can be chosen for your slideshow – Apple Music cannot be used.

When you have finished setting up your Slideshow, just click the **Play Slideshow** button to enjoy your slideshow!

You will also find the '**Play Slideshow**' option when you right-click (or two-finger-click) on an album or folder.

Creating a more customised slideshow

It is also possible to create a 'saved slideshow' Project, which allows for the re-ordering of photos, different transitions, text slides and captions and more.

The best way to create a Saved Slideshow is to first create an Album that contains the photos that you want to include in your Slideshow.

Then, just right-click (or two-finger-click) on the album in the sidebar or on the thumbnail of the album, and choose **Create**, then **Slideshow**.

This will create a slideshow Project in the **Projects** section and give the this project the same name as the Album. It will include all the photos that are in the Album.

A slideshow project can also be created from a set of selected photos. Again, just right-click (or two-finger-click) on the selection to see the **Create** option, the **Slideshow**.

There are lots of additional options for then customising this Slideshow 'project'. Why not give it a go?!

Importing Photos into your Photos Library

There is a variety of ways to get photos into your Photos library. Some, like iCloud Photos and My Photo Stream (discussed later) happen automatically. Others involve imports from external devices, or files and apps on the Mac.

Import Photos from an iPhone, iPad or iPod Touch

Using the cable that came with the Apple mobile device, connect the device to the USB port on your computer.

If the iDevice is not on, turn it on. Make sure you unlock it with your passcode.

If the iDevice pops up a message asking if the device should 'Trust' the computer, confirm the **Trust** option. You may also be asked to enter your device's passcode to confirm that the computer can be trusted.

The **Photos** app should open automatically. If it doesn't, click the **Photos** app in the Dock to open it.

The photos and videos on the device will be analysed, and you will be shown which are already in the Photos library (the **Already Imported** section), and those that are not yet in the Photos library (in the **New Photos** section).

- Import only some photos – click the photos you want to import, then choose the **Import Selected** button.

- Import all new photos from your camera - click the **Import All New Photos** button to do this.

57

Importing Photos into your Photos Library

Before you Import

There another thing to decide before you click either of the **Import** buttons.

Since MacOS High Sierra, it has been possible to choose to import the photos to a specific album – either a new album or an existing album. Click the down-arrow of the **Import to** field to see the list of options.

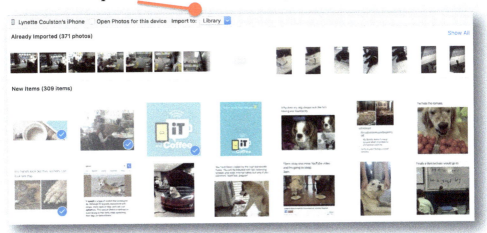

If no choice is made here for an 'import to' album, the set of imported photos will still be able to be viewed in the **Imports** view – and, if needed, selected and added to an album at some point after the import.

If the Photos app did not open automatically when you plugged in the mobile device, tick the '**Open Photos for this Device**' option at the top to ensure that the Photos app automatically opens next time the device is plugged in.

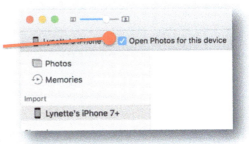

After the import process is finished, it is safe to disconnect the mobile device's USB cable without the need to 'eject' it.

An important note about Imports

Only photo imports that you give you the 'Import' review screen will go to the **Imports** album.

Importing Photos into your Photos Library

Import photos from a digital camera

Using the cable that came with the camera, connect the camera to the USB port on your computer. (If your Mac has an SD card slot or you have a card reader, you can insert the SD card into that slot.)

For a connected camera, if the camera is not on, turn it on, and make sure it is set to the correct mode for importing photos. For information on which mode to choose, see the instructions provided with your camera.

If your camera has a "sleep" mode, make sure it is disabled or set to a time increment long enough to allow your images to download.

Open the Photos app, if it is not already open or it does not open automatically.

The import process is then the same as described for your Apple mobile device.

With SD cards and cameras connected to the Mac using a USB cable, make sure you safely eject before removing the card/cable. Click on the symbol on the right of the device in Finder to do this.

Import photos from internal/external storage

If you have photos saved on your computer's hard drive (if, for example, you scanned photos or downloaded photos from an email), you can import them into Photos.

The same applies if the files are on a USB Flash drive (USB stick) or an external portable hard disk drive.

Importing can be achieved in a few ways

Method 1: With both the Finder and Photos visible, drag one or more photos or a folder of photos from the Finder onto the Photos option in the Photos app's sidebar, or onto an album that you have created.

If duplicates are detected, you will be asked if you want to continue importing the photos or to 'skip' duplicates. Choose 'Apply to all duplicates' if you wish your choice to apply to all imports.

59

Importing Photos into your Photos Library

Method 2:   Drag one or more photos or a folder of photos from the Finder to on top of the Photos icon in the dock.

Method 3:   In Photos, choose **File->Import...**, then find and select the photos you want to import, then and click **Review for Import**.

Methods 2 and 3 two will give a similar 'Import' screen to that which applied for mobile device and camera imports.

Once again, choose to import all new photos, or select a subset and **Import Selected**.

In this scenario, you will also notice a new checkbox, **Keep Folder Organised,** below the 'Import' buttons.

If this checkbox is ticked, the photos that you import will retain the folder structure that existed in Finder.

As an example, importing a Finder folder with 3 sub-folders (image on right) results in the creation of equivalent folder and sub-folders in the My Albums area of Photos, with the albums given the same name as the folder holding the photos (bottom image on right).

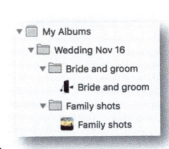

This is a great feature (added in MacOS High Sierra) for anyone who has already organised their photos into folders on either Windows or a Mac, and who wants to keep that same organisation when the photos are imported to the Photos app, as folders and albums in Photos.

Importing Photos into your Photos Library

Choose whether to store photos in the Photos Library when Importing

Before you import the photos from your Mac or external storage device, you can choose whether you want your photos actually stored in your Photos Library.

This is done in the Photos Preferences.

➢ Go to **Photos->Preferences-> General**

➢ Tick or untick the '**Copy items to the iPhoto Library**'.

If you choose not to copy the photos to the Photos Library, they will be left in their original location and the Photo Library 'database' will know to look for them there (instead of in the photo library where they would normally 'live').

In this case, the 'source' of the photos must be available when you use the Photos app. If that source is an external storage device, the device must be plugged in and available.

One key limitation of choosing to <u>not</u> copy the photos into the Photos library relates to iCloud Photos. Photos that are stored outside the Photos library **cannot be sync'd to iCloud Photos**.

If you choose to **Copy items to the Photos Library**, you can then choose later to delete the copied photos from the original location (unless you really want to keep them as a backup in that other location).

Save Photos directly from email, Message, or web page

A photo received in a mail message can be directly exported to Photos'Right- click' (or two-finger-click) on the photo (or select more than one by holding the Command key as you click the photos) and choose the **Export to Photos** option.

The same applies for photos in your Messages – except the option is **Add to Photos Library**

Importing Photos into your Photos Library

Similarly for web pages, photos you find in Safari may also be able to be saved to your Photos library.

Right-click (or two-finger-click) on a web page's photo, and (if it is available) choose the **Add Image to Photos** option.

You will then be able to find any photo that you add in this manner as the last in the **Photos** album.

They will appear in the **Moments, Collections** and **Years** timelines according to the date and time information recorded against each photo.

Where do my photos 'live'?

The photos you see in your Photos App are held in a special file that usually lives in your **Pictures** folder on your Mac. Open **Finder** to see this folder

You may not see the **Pictures** folder in your **Finder** sidebar.

If it is not there, visit **Finder's Preferences.**

Click the **Sidebar** option along the top and ensure the **Pictures** item is ticked.

(While you are there, turn on any other folders that you want to see as your Favourites in the Finder sidebar.)

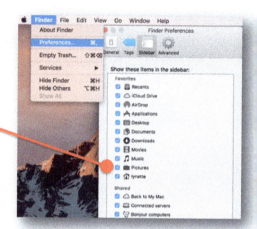

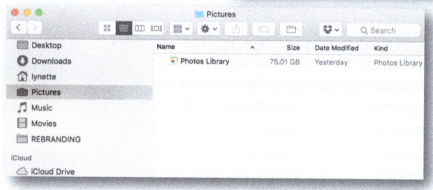

In the Pictures folder is a special file called **Photos Library.photoslibrary** (or you may see it as **Photos Library),** which contains your Photos Library and its database.

Whenever you open the Photos app in the Dock, it will look for this special file and show you its contents.

Double-clicking on the **Photos Library** file in Pictures will also open that library using your Photos App.

Where do my photos 'live'

Storing your Photos Library elsewhere

In saying that Pictures is the usual location of the Photos Library, this library does not have to 'live' in this particular location.

In fact, your Photos Library could be stored anywhere on your Mac, or even on an External Hard Disk Drive.

This can be especially handy if you don't have much storage capacity on your Mac and want to keep your photos stored elsewhere.

More than one Photos Library

You can even have more than one **Photos Library**, and can open any alternative Photos Library by simply double-clicking on the applicable **Photos Library** file in Finder

Your Photos app will 'remember' which library was last opened and will open the same one again if the Photos app is selected from the Dock.

If you do have more than one Photo Library, only one library can be the 'main' library used as your 'system' library and by your iCloud.

In **Photos -> Preferences**, the **General** option (top left) shows the location of the **Photos Library** you are currently using.

If the current library is not the 'system' photo library, you do have the option to make this alternative library into the main library by choosing **Use as System Photo Library** (which will be available if you are currently viewing an alternate photo library).

Be very careful about changing this though! If you have been sync'ing with iCloud, you will be messing around with this, something you may not wish to do!

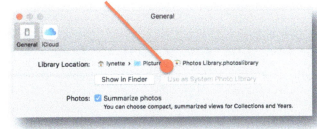

Editing Photos

What sort of Editing is possible?

Quite often, the photos that we take can be made so much better with some minor (or major!) adjustments.

The following editing capabilities are provided by the Photos app on your iPad and iPhone:

- Adjust the colour, light, and various other aspects of the photo including retouching and removing red eyes.

- Apply a range of filters to enhance your photo and change its 'look'

- Crop and adjust alignment

- Rotate

- Auto enhance

- Other edits using 'Extensions' from other apps.

We will look at each of these editing features in turn shortly.

Before we talk about the editing options, it is important to note that the edited photo does not replace the original photo. Your edited photo can be reverted to its original state at any time.

How do I get to the editing options?

When you are viewing an individual photo, you will see the **Edit** option at the top right of the screen. (In MacOS Sierra, the symbol was   ).

Editing Photos

Just select any of the editing options to make the necessary changes to your Photo and choose **Done** at top right when you have completed editing.

Once you have applied any of these editing options, you will notice the **Revert to Original** option appears at top left, to allow you to go back to your un-edited version of the photo at any time.

Along the top of the Edit screen is a toolbar. We'll first look at the **Adjust**, **Filters** and **Crop** options.

Adjust

Clicking on the **Adjust** option gives a long list of options on the right-hand side of the screen, as shown in the image on the right.

These options allow you to adjust lighting, colour, remove flaws, correct 'red-eye' and more.

On the left-hand side of each edit option is a ▶ that can be clicked to expand that edit option.

For **Light, Colour** and **Black & White** options, you will see a 'slider' that allows for the manual adjustment of this aspect of the image.

Simply drag the vertical bar to adjust the lighting level, colour level or black & white level up and down.

For more 'granular' adjustments, choose the 'down-arrow' next to the word **Options**, which appears for each of these first three options.

Editing Photos

Once you have adjusted any of these settings, a tick will appear on the right of the applicable adjustment.

To disable an adjustment, just remove this tick. Re-apply the adjustment by ticking again – and your previous adjustments will be remembered. To reset any of the adjustments, click the 'back-arrow' that appears on the left of the tick.

I'll leave those of you who are more advanced photo editors to have a play with these options and work out what they all do!

For those of you looking for easy adjustments to your photo, choose the **Auto** setting for each adjustment type and see the effect it has. You can always use Command-Z to undo the applied adjustment.

You can also 'untick' the blue circle on the right of each adjustment type to remove, then re-apply the adjustment – to see if you are happy with the 'look' it gives.

Retouch

I love this one! Retouch allows you to remove unwanted objects or defects from your photo. It can even help smooth out those wrinkles! Have a play with this option to get the hang of it!

Here is an example of a photo that I have quickly and easily 'retouched' to remove the dog and the school badge.

Editing Photos

Expand the **Retouch** option by clicking the ▸.

You will see a **Size** slider, which allows you to set the size of the 'dot' ◯ that you will use to retouch your photos.

In the example on the previous page, I set the slider to about midway (to give a medium sized circle), then first 'Option-clicked' on the couch area above the dog.

This set the replacement 'dot' that would be used when I clicked and dragged over the dog. I had to click and drag a few times to get the required effect.

I then did the same thing with the jumper, option-clicking on a blue patch of jumper then clicking several times on the jumper logo to remove it.

In the below photo, you see the instructions that appear, then disappear for the 'retouch' option.

Click & drag over spots to remove.
Option-click to choose the source area.

Editing Photos

Red Eye

We've all seen those photos taken with a flash, where the person in the shot looks like they are possessed – with red eye/s.

Your Mac allows you to remove red eyes from photos really easily.

Just click on ▸ on left of **Red Eye** and you will see some additional options, as shown on the right.

My favourite is the **Auto** option, which will automatically detect and remove any red eye issues in the photo.

If you are not happy with the Auto results, adjust the slider to approximate the size of the red eye, and click on each of the problem eyes to see if you get a better result.

Hopefully your subject won't end up looking too demonic!

Other adjustments

The Photos app includes a wide range of other adjustments – white balance, levels, curves, selective colour, definition, noise reduction, sharpen and vignette. I won't go through what each of these means and does – but those of you who are avid photographers will hopefully be familiar with these options and what they do.

Editing Photos

Editing Photos

Filters

Filters provides a way of changing the colours and tones of your image with a number of special effects, such as black and white, faded, a 'polaroid' look, and a few others.

Click on **Filters** (at top) to see the different options available on the right.

To choose a different effect for your photo, just click on one of the filters.

If you like that 'look' and wish the save the photo with this new effect, click **Done** at the top right.

To put your photo back to its original, unfiltered look, choose the **Original** filter at the top of the list.

Crop

The **Crop** feature of Edit mode allows you the change the borders of the photo – to cut out part of the photo or zoom in on the main area of interest.

It also allows for the straightening of your photo, or 'flipping'.

Click on **Crop** and you will see a border appear with 'tabs' at each corner.

You will also notice a 'wheel' on the right of the image that can be used to adjust the angle of the photo.

Editing Photos

Just drag wheel up and down to 'turn' this wheel and adjust the angle of the photo.

To crop the photo, simply drag the corners. You can then move the photo around within the adjusted 'frame' to adjust the positioning of the photo's features.

Something to thing to consider before you crop is whether you want to maintain the same '**Aspect ratio**' for the image – which means keeping or changing the shape and proportions.

To adjust this, just click **Aspect** to see the set of options shown on the right.

Choose the required Aspect. **Original** will set the proportions based on the original size (i.e. if it was a standard 4x6 photo, the shape will be adjusted accordingly).

Drag the photo around within the new framed area to adjust the positioning of the features of the photo within the frame.

At any point, the changes can be undone using the **Reset** option at the bottom.

Use the Auto button at the bottom to automatically straighten a crooked image.

To complete any cropping and/or straightening you have applied, choose **Done** at top right.

Editing Photos

More options

There are a few other options available in Edit mode, and these are found on the top right-hand side of the edit screen, to the left of the **Done** options.

Quick Enhance

The **Quick Enhance** mnd can provide a quick-fix for a not-so-great photo.

It balances the darks and lights and improves the contrast and brightness.

Just click on the magic wand symbol on the left of the **Done** option to see what a difference it makes.

Click it again to 'undo' this quick enhancement

Rotate

You will sometimes find that your photo has the wrong 'orientation', so is not able to be viewed in full screen mode or requires you to stand on your head to view it!

Click on the **Rotate** option to rotate the image 90° anti-clockwise. Keep clicking **Rotate** until your image is oriented correctly.

Extensions

For most Mac users, clicking on the extensions option will only give options **Markup** and **More...**

If you have any photo editing apps on your Mac, the **More** option will allow you to access any 'extensions' (i.e. a set of tools) that those apps provide for the Photos app.

Markup is a very handy option (added in MacOS Sierra) that allows you to 'draw on' an image, add a text box, and perform various other 'markup' operations.

Choose **Save Changes** when you are done.

Editing Photos

Compare your 'before' and 'after'

Once you have edited your photo in any way, you will see another option that appears just to the right of the traffic lights.

Click and hold on ▣□ to see the image before you applied the changes.

Let go to see the 'after' again.

If you are not happy with what you have done, choose **Revert to Original** on the right of that symbol.

Viewing and changing information about your Photo

It can be very useful to view the information about your photos, to find out things like

- The size of your photo
- When it was taken
- What device took it
- Location
- Identified people in photos

It is even possible to adjust date, time and location data stored against a photo. All of this information is known as the 'metadata' of the photo.

Let's look at the ways you can view and edit this 'metadata'.

The Info option

While viewing an individual photo, you will see the ⓘ option in the set of options at the top right.

Click this symbol, or right-click (two-finger-click) on any photo and choose **Get Info**.

The metadata associated with the photo or video is shown in a separate window, including a map with the photo location (if this information is stored against the photo's).

If any 'faces' are found in the photo, you will have the chance to allocate a name to each face (for any that don't yet have a name).

Also available are some fields that can be added and edited by you - Title, Description, Keywords, faces.

Including these pieces of additional information about your photos and videos provides further ways of viewing, searching and organizing your photos and videos

Viewing and changing information about your Photo

Identify Faces in a photo

Choosing the + option in the Faces section of the info screen will add a new 'circle' to your photo, one that can be placed over the face of an unidentified person, and then allocated a name. (We covered the People album earlier in this guide.)

Add or change a photo's location

Location information can be added later to any photo or video - very useful if you forgot to turn on Location Services on your iPhone or iPad, or if your camera does not have GPS capability.

In the Info view, click **Assign a Location** and then start typing the location – city, street address, country or attraction. You will see suggestions from Maps appear – select the one that applies to your photo or video.

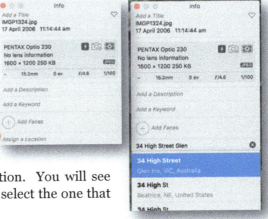

This will then allow your photo (or video) to be shown on a map, in the Places album, and in other areas of your Photos app that show maps.

Viewing and changing information about your Photo

Changing a Photo's date and time

In some situations, it is desirable to modify the date/time information stored about a photo (or a video).

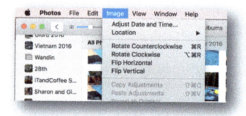

To do this, select the applicable photo (or several photos) and then choose (from the main menu)

Image -> Adjust Date and Time

This will show a screen that allows the adjusted time to be set, as well as the time zone applicable to the photo.

It is important to note that the original details of the photo are not lost when this is done and can be restored at any point if required.

This edit option is great for old hard-copy photos that you scanned into digital format, and that have the 'date scanned' as their adjusted date.

Setting an adjusted date that is closer to the date the photo was taken will allow them to appear in the correct year/month/day of your timeline.

Trimming Videos

The videos that you stored in your Photos library can be very easily trimmed, to remove unneeded footage from the start or end.

When the cursor is hovered over the video, you will see a bar with various symbols.

In particular, you will see the 'settings' symbol. Clicking on this will reveal a set of options, one of which is the **Trim** option.

Click **Trim** to see a film strip like that shown below, with a yellow band around it.

Just drag the left edge of the bar to the right and/or the right edge of the bar to the left to trim the start and end.

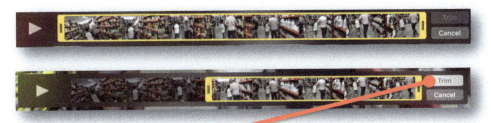

Once you are finished, choose **Trim** to complete the trimming process. Easy!

If you decide that you want your untrimmed video back, just click the symbol again, and choose the **Reset Trim** option (which will be available if there has been a trim performed previously).

Duplicating photos and videos

On occasion, it may be necessary the take a copy of a photo – perhaps before you apply some edits, so that you can keep both the edited and unedited versions of the photo side by side.

First select one or more photos using the method described earlier in the guide.

When one or more photo/s is selected, you will find the **Duplicate** option as follows:

- Choose **File->Duplicate n Photo(s)**

- Right-click (or two-finger-click on the selected photo/s) and choose **Duplicate n Photo(s)**

The duplicated photo/s will keep the same date/s, time and location information as the original/s.

Albums and Folders can be duplicated too

If you ever need to duplicate an album or folder that you have created, just right-click (two-finger-click) on it and choose the **Duplicate** option that appears in the list.

Searching for photos

When you are viewing thumbnails of photos (i.e. you are not viewing an individual photo), there will always be a **Search** field showing at the top right.

This **Search** feature allows for searching for photos/videos based on a wide range of search criteria.

- Place

- Person/Face

- Date or Date range

- Keyword, Title, Description (if you have any of this user-specified data recorded against your photos)

- Category - eg Christmas Tree, Tree, Water, Dog, Cat, (new in OS X Sierra)

Below, you can see what I get if I type the letters 'dog' into my search field – a set of photos with dogs, Moments that include dogs, Albums referring to dogs, a variety of categories for dog, and places. Choose **See All** at the top right of some of the sections on this screen to view all photos represented by the section.

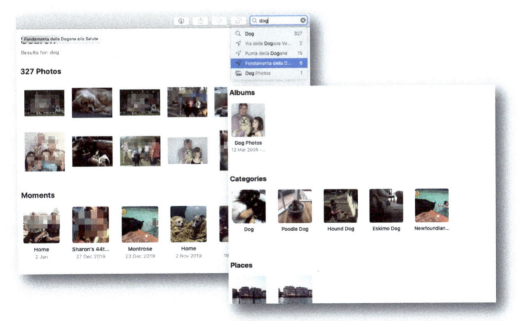

Searching for photos

Having found a set of photos that match your search criteria, you can then quickly create an album containing the photos that match.

Such an album can then be used as part of the rules for a Smart Album (see next section).

Organising your Photos -
Smart Albums

We have previously covered how to create your own Albums of photos – and how to go about adding photos to those albums.

These standard albums only contain the photos that you choose to put into the album.

There is another type of album that can be created, one that can determine its contents automatically based on a set of 'rules' that you define.

These are called **Smart Albums**.

Creating a Smart Album

As an example, you could set up a Smart Album that includes all videos that were taken in a date range.

To create a Smart Album, choose
File -> New Smart Album.

You will see the following screen, where the rule or rules for your Smart Album can be defined.

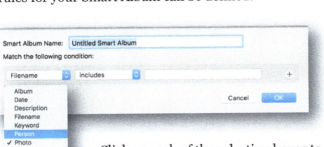

Give your Smart Album a name in the first field, then choose the first condition.

Click on each of the selection boxes to choose the basis of your rule – on the left is the list of attributes that can be used for the rule.

In my case, I will set up my first condition to look for 'photos' that have type 'movie', and the second condition to look for items with a 'date' in the past 6 months.

82

Organising your Photos - Smart Albums

I chose the + symbol on right of the first conditions to create a second condition. If I need to remove a condition, I use the -.)

I have also set my rule to require that 'all' of the conditions are true for a photo to be included (instead of 'any').

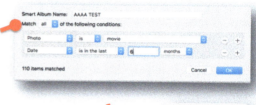

Once I choose OK, a new Smart Album will appear in my Albums area, with the chosen name.

Viewing Smart Albums

Smart Albums are listed in your set of Albums, and are indicated by the symbol on the left side

The contents of the Smart Album are determined by the rule, so it is not possible to 'drag' or manually add photos to the Smart Album.

The Smart Album's contents will change dynamically based on the photos that are currently in your library – those that meet the Smart Album's rule/s will be automatically added.

If a photo that was previously in the Smart Album is deleted, it will be automatically deleted from the Smart Album.

Sorting, editing, duplicating, and deleting a Smart Album

Various options relating to the Smart Album are available by right-clicking (two-finger-clicking) on the album.

Choose **Edit Smart Album** to change the album's rules.

The name can also be changed in the same way, by choosing the **Rename Smart Album** option.

Sort the contents of the Smart Album using the Sort option. And, of course you can **Duplicate** and **Delete** the Smart Album.

Exporting Photos

On occasion, you may find it is necessary to export a set of photos from your Photos app – say to a USB stick or external hard drive.

Exporting of a selection of photos can be achieved as follows:

- Select your photos

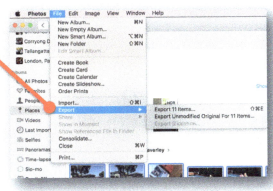

- Choose **File –> Export**

- You will see there is the option to '**Export xx Items ...**' or to '**Export unmodified Original for xx items...**'.

- The first option will export the 'modified' version of your photo/s, including any edits, face allocations, adjustments to date/time and location, and any title/description/keyword additions.

- Each photo will retain the 'date and time taken' metadata associated with each photo/video, **BUT** the 'date created' and 'date modified' showing in Finder for each image file will be the date and time that the export occurred. This can be very frustrating.

- If you want to keep the date/time that the photo/video was taken in Finder, you will need to choose the second option - '**Export unmodified Original for xx items...**'. The disadvantage of this option is that any edits you have applied to your photo will not be included in the exported photo/s and video/s.

For the **Export xx Items ...** option you will see the screen on the right.

If you want to include Location information with the exported photos, tick the 'Location Information' option.

Exporting Photos

Choose **Export** when you are ready to choose the disk location for the exported items.

You will then see the standard Finder 'Save' screen, that allows you to choose where to save your exported photos/videos.

You can even create a New Folder in which to store the items.

Once you have chosen the location, click the **Export** button.

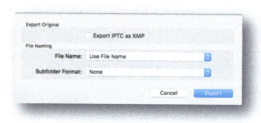

A slightly different, simpler export screen (right) appears if you chose the second option, **Export unmodified Original for xx items...**

Select **Export**, to again get the Finder 'Save' screen and complete the export process of the original versions of the photos.

Handy tip for exporting a selection of photos

If you have a random selection to export, it is best to set up an Album first.

Once your album is complete, click on a single photo or video 'thumbnail', then press **Command-A** to select all photos in the Album

Then choose **File -> Export**, and follow the steps described above.

Remember, if you Export the 'unmodified' photos, your photos keep date information when viewed in Finder.

Sorting out all those Duplicates

It is certainly not unusual to find yourself with lots of duplicate photos in your Photos Library.

Unfortunately, Apple doesn't provide any built-in capability to search for duplicates.

The best way to search for duplicates manually is to use the Photos 'timeline' view, where you will see any situations where you have the same photos side-by-side.

But this can be very tedious.

Another option is to purchase a 3rd-party product that allows you to sort out all those duplicates a lot more quickly.

I have purchased a product called **Photo Sweeper,** available in the Mac App Store. This has served me very well in my quest to rid my library of the duplicates that creep in there on a regular basis.

Of course, there are many other products that do the same thing, and this guide is not seeking to recommend any one product.

Your best bet is to Google reviews of products that manage duplicated photos on a Mac – and make your own assessment and purchase.

Melbourne readers can always visit iTandCoffee for one-on-one assistance with resolving duplicate photos.

Photo Books

From 2002 up until 2018, there was the option to create a **Photo Book** within the **Photos App**. These photo books were printed by Apple.

As of the end of September 2018, Apple is no longer in the business of printing Photo Books.

The option to create a photo book is still available within the Photos app, but you will now have to install and use a third-party a photo book app from the **App Store**.

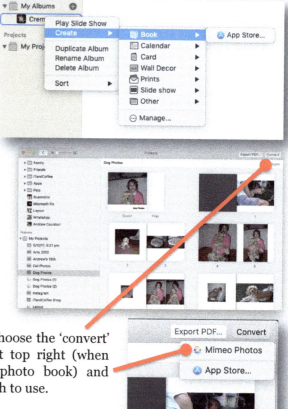

Selecting the option to create a book will redirect you to the App Store to choose an app.

As at the time of writing this guide, the only app available in Australia is **Mimeo Photos.**

We won't go into detail in this guide about how to use any third-party product.

However, it is good to know that, if you have already started a Photo Book, it is possible to choose the 'convert' option and choose **Convert** at top right (when viewing your already-created photo book) and choose the 3rd-party app you wish to use.

Alternatively, there are many other non-Apple services for creating photo books – Snapfish, Blurb, Albumworks and Momento, just to name a few.

To create a card or calendar, or order prints:

The same Applies for other printed products that you used to be able to order from Apple. These must now be created and ordered through a third-party provider.

Now let's talk about Photos in iCloud

There are three aspects of iCloud that relate to your photos and videos. These are

- iCloud Photos
- My Photo Stream
- Shared Albums

For any of these options to be available in the Photos app, your Mac must be using iCloud.

To check if you are signed in to iCloud, go to your **System Preferences**.

 -> **System Preferences** -> **Apple ID**

Managing the various aspects of photos in iCloud can be done from the **Photos** app.

Go to **Photos -> Preferences** and choose the **iCloud** option (at the top) to see the set of options in relation to iCloud.

Next is a summary of what each of the three main iCloud Photos options offer.

We will then cover each of these areas in further detail in the next few sections of the guide.

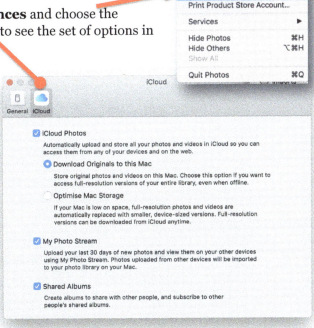

Now let's talk about Photos in iCloud

iCloud Photos

Stores all your photos in iCloud and allows each of your devices to view and manage this same set of photos and Albums.

Extra iCloud storage may be needed to store large libraries, and devices that can't fit the entire library will need internet access when viewing any photos. (Note. Windows computers can also use iCloud Photos.)

My Photo Stream

Allows streaming of photos (not videos) between your iCloud-enabled devices, including Windows computers, whenever those devices are connected to Wi-Fi.

My Photo Stream photos are only held in iCloud for 30 days, and only the last 1000 Photo Stream photos are stored on your Apple mobile devices.

My Photo Stream DOES NOT offer permanent storage of your photos in iCloud.

If you don't see the My Photo Stream option in your Preferences, it is because this feature is no longer available for newer iCloud accounts (as Apple is wanting people to use iCloud Photos instead).

Shared Albums

Allows creation of albums in iCloud, that can be then shared with other people.

These Shared Albums are separate to your iCloud Photos – so deleting a photo from your library will not delete it from any Shared Album (and vice-versa) you have added it to.

The great news is that Shared Albums do not add to your iCloud storage usage. A Shared Album can have up to 5000 items in it.

iCloud Photos

iCloud Photos was introduced in 2015. It provides centralised storage of all your photos in iCloud and allows the viewing and updating of the 'library' in iCloud from any devices connected to that iCloud account.

The great benefit of iCloud Photos

Photos and albums are synchronized between all Apple devices that are connected to the iCloud Photos – meaning that albums can be created on an iPhone, iPad and Mac, and be visible then on all other devices.

It also means that photos deleted on one device are also deleted on other devices. People albums sync, as do Favourites.

For many people (and I am one of them!), this offers a great solution to storage of their photos.

The disadvantages of iCloud Photos

The problems start when your Photos library is a large one.

iCloud Photos offers only an 'all or nothing' solution to storage of your photos on each device. This means that, if iCloud Photos is turned on, the device will show EVERY photo and video that is in the library.

If your library is big, it may not fit on your mobile devices. It may not fit on your Macbook if it has only 128GB or 256GB of storage.

In this case, your device will store 'cut down' versions of your photos – versions that are 'blurry' and can only be viewed properly once they are downloaded from your iCloud.

In this case, you need internet access to view your photos, and have to endure a delay before you can see full resolution versions of your photos and videos.

This can result in unexpected mobile data usage, and great frustration at the delay in seeing a clear image, or at not being able to view photos when there is no internet.

If your iCloud Photos library does not fit on a device, the photo storage must be 'optimised'.

This is one of the options a that can be selected in **Photos -> Preferences**, in the **iCloud** option.

iCloud Photos

Added to all this is the cost of storing all your photos in iCloud. If your Photos library is large, you will be looking at a higher iCloud subscription cost of $4.49 per month for 200GB or perhaps $14.99 per month for 2TB. (Australian $ shown here.)

Should you use iCloud Photos?

At the time of writing this guide, iTandCoffee's recommendation is that you don't set up iCloud Photos unless you are fully aware of the implications – especially if your devices don't have a lot of available storage capacity.

If iCloud Photos has been accidentally enabled, it can be tricky to undo – especially where you don't use iCloud Photo Library on your computer and want to import (using a USB cable) the photos from your iPhone or iPad.

You may find that the import process shows there are no photos to be imported, even though you know there should be.

The problem is that iCloud has the photos, but your mobile device only has the 'optimised' version of the photos (which can't be imported to the computer).

Refer later in this guide for details of what to do if your photos are in iCloud and you need to get them out of iCloud and onto your Mac.

My Photo Stream

My Photo Stream is part of iCloud – a feature that you can choose to enable on each of your Apple devices.

*(**Important Note.** If you are using iCloud Photos, you won't need to use My Photo Stream unless you have a device that is not yet using iCloud Photos. If you have a newer iCloud account, this feature may not be available to you.)*

My Photo Stream's purpose is to allow streaming of photos (not videos) between your Photo Stream-enabled devices.

If your iPad or iPhone has this feature turned 'on', photos you take on that device will be uploaded to iCloud for 30 days. A Wi-Fi connection is required for this upload to occur.

If the feature is turned 'on' in your iCloud settings on the Mac, photos found in your **My Photo Stream** in iCloud will automatically download to your Mac when it is connected to the internet.

When you open your Photos app, the already downloaded Photo Stream photos will then be imported into your Photos Library. They may take a little while to appear.

The **My Photo Stream** album in the Photos App shows the photos that appear in your Photo Stream. *(Note. As mentioned earlier, the My Photo Stream album is not present in Photos if iCloud Photos is turned On.)*

To turn on your **My Photo Stream** in Photos on your Mac, go to **Photos -> Preferences -> iCloud -> My Photo Stream.** Ensure this option is ticked.

An important thing to remember is that, while any photos imported to your Mac via My Photo Stream will remain on you Mac until you delete them, the My Photo Stream album on the iPhone and iPad will only ever hold a maximum of 1000 photos.

Older photos will disappear from the My Photo Stream album on those mobile devices once you reach 1000.

iCloud Shared Albums

Sharing your photos using iCloud

A set of photos can be shared using your iCloud, by setting up **Shared Albums.**

Shared Albums allow you to share an album of photos with other iCloud users, and with other 'non-Apple' people – without using any additional iCloud storage allocation. Shared Albums can have up to 5000 photos or videos.

I use iCloud Shared Albums all the time to share photos of trips, family events and more.

Those who share the album with you can like, comment, or even add more photos to the Shared Album.

For this option to be available, you must ensure the following setup has occurred:

• Sign in to iCloud on your Mac - this is done in **System Preferences -> Apple ID**

• Turn 'on' **Shared Albums** from **Photos -> Preferences -> iCloud**

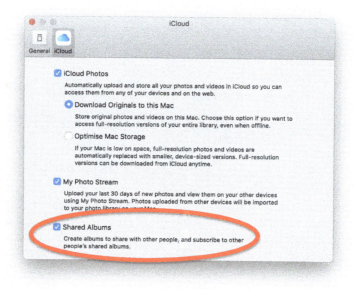

iCloud Shared Albums

Having ensured that your Shared Albums option is active, it is then easy to share a set of photos via your iCloud.

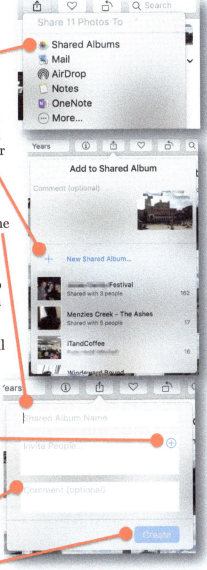

- Select one or more photos (using the technique described earlier)

- Choose the Share symbol ⬆️

- Choose the option **Shared Albums**

- Choose the existing Shared Album to which to add the photos – ie choose an existing Shared iCloud Album from the list shown or create a New Shared Album

- For a **New Shared Album**

  ○ In **Shared Album Name**, assign a name to the album,

  ○ In **Invite People**, enter the names of Contacts (they must be iCloud users who have also turned on the **Shared Album** option).

    As you start typing a contact name, it will appear in 'blue' if the contact is on iCloud.

    Alternatively, choose the blue + to see your Contacts list and choose the applicable (and iCloud-enabled) Contacts.

    You can skip inviting people at this point, and do it later instead.

  ○ Add a **Comment** if you like

  ○ Select **Create** after you have selected all the required contacts that you would like to share with (if any).

iCloud Shared Albums

Viewing Shared Albums

You can then view your Shared Albums in the **Shared** area of Photos.

If you don't see anything listed in the Shared area, hover the mouse pointer over the word **Shared** so that the word **Show** appears, then click this **Show** option.

The **Shared** area of your Photos app shows those albums you shared with others and those that are shared with you.

The Activity option shows last added photos, comments and likes for all Shared Albums.

Permanently saving photos from a Shared iCloud Album

Photos you see in the **Shared Albums** area are separate to those in the main Photos library. They are not permanently stored on your device and will disappear if the Shared Album is deleted or you 'unsubscribe' (see later in this section).

If you wish to permanently save photos that you have in the Shared area, you need to **Import** them to your Photos library. (Only then can they be used in your Albums.)

Select the Shared photos you wish to import (using the selection method described earlier in this guide).

Right Click (or two-finger-click) on one of the selected photos and choose **Import**.

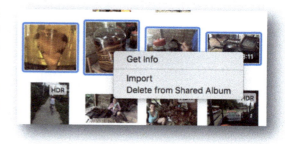

iCloud Shared Albums

Adding photos or videos to a Shared Album

To add new photos to a Shared Album, select the Shared album then choose **Add photos and videos.**

The added photos will then appear as the last few photos in your All Photos album (until you add more photos, that is).

Alternatively, use the same method described earlier – of selecting the photos first, then choosing the **Share** symbol⬆ and the **Shared Albums** option.

Click on an existing Shared Album to add the selected photos to that album.

Managing who can see your Shared Album

Add new subscribers to a Shared Album at any time by choosing the 'Person' symbol at top right. This symbol is visible when you select a Shared Album in the sidebar.

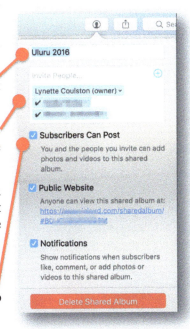

Change the name of the Shared album in the first field of the window that appears.

The + symbol in the 'Invite People' frame allows additional people to be invited to subscribe to the album.

If there is someone you want to remove as a subscriber, just click the 'down-arrow' on the right of their name and choose the option 'Remove Subscriber'

You will see several other options in this screen

- Choose whether subscribers can add photos to the shared albums (**Subscribers can Post**)

iCloud Shared Albums

- Option to create a '**Public Website**' that can be shared. This generates a link to a web page that will show your Shared iCloud Album's photos, a link that can be shared with those who don't use Apple or iCloud. Your iCloud album can then be viewed in any web browser using the shared link

- Choose whether you want **Notifications** popping up on your Mac about any activity in relation to album

Unsubscribing from an album someone else shared with you

If you no longer wish to see a Shared Album that someone else shared with you, just right-click (or two-finger-click) on it and choose **Unsubscribe**.

This will remove the album from the Shared area on all your devices.

Special 'Family' Shared Album

If you are part of an iCloud Family, a special Shared Album automatically appears in the Shared list. It is called **Family**.

As you would guess, it is designed for sharing photos with other members of your iCloud Family.

Deleting a Shared Album

If you no longer want to keep a Shared Album that you created, right-click and choose **Delete**.

Alternatively, choose ⓘ and select the **Delete Shared Album** option at the bottom of the window.

The Shared Album will be removed from the Shared area on all your devices.

Deleted shared albums also disappear from Shared area of any subscribers

How to get your Photos out of iCloud

If you have turned on **iCloud Photos** on your iPhone (or iPad), but not on your Mac (or Windows computer), you may find yourself in the situation where your photos are no longer stored on your mobile device - that they have been 'sucked up' into **iCloud Photos** instead.

As described earlier, this occurs in cases where there is insufficient room to store the photos on your mobile device, resulting in an 'optimised' **Photos** library on the device. When you view your photos, they must be downloaded from iCloud - requiring internet access, and often resulting in a delay before you can view your full resolution photo.

Another consequence of an optimised Photos library on the i-Device may be that, when you plug your iPhone (or iPad) into your computer, you may be told that there are no photos to import - even though you know that you just took some new photos!

The problem is that they have been uploaded to iCloud and removed from the device to save space, before you can import them.

This can leave your photos in a 'no-man's-land', where they are not on your iPhone/iPad, and are not on your computer.

In this case, most people I see with this problem would choose to turn off the iCloud Photo Library option on their mobile device - so that they have more control over which photos are actually stored on their device, and don't have to rely on internet access to be able to view their photos.

The problem then is how to get the photos, that are then only stored in iCloud Photo Library, out of iCloud and onto their computer.

Before we look at options ...

Apple provides the **icloud.com** website, where you are able to sees the content of your iCloud - including the content of your iCloud Photos.

You would think that logging into **icloud.com** would solve your problem - ie. that you would be able to export your photos from there.

Unfortunately, there is currently no option to 'download all' photos. You can only download up to 1000 photos at a time. If you have a large number of photos to download, this may not offer a workable solution.

How to get your Photos out of iCloud

Turn on iCloud Photos in Photos on your Mac

On the Mac, you could turn on **iCloud Photo Library** in the **Photos** app's preferences (or in **System Preferences -> iCloud -> Photos**) to get your iCloud-based photos downloaded to your computer.

In many cases, however, this is not the best idea.

If you already have a big photos library on your Mac, that library will first be uploaded to iCloud, perhaps requiring additional iCloud storage and, in many cases, a lot of time to complete the upload.

If you are not wanting to continue using iCloud Photo Library, you may want to get your photos out of iCloud without having to involve your current Photos Library.

A solution that doesn't involve uploading existing Photos Library

If you don't want to involve your current Photos Library, the best option is the create a second Photos Library and use it to get your photos out of iCloud.

Once the photos are downloaded to this second library, you can use the Export option to extract the photos and then Import them to the 'real' Photos Library.

Set up a second Photos Library

Setting up a second Photos Library is quite straight-forward.

Make sure your Photos app is closed. Then, as you click the **Photos** app, hold down the **Option** key.

This will provide the **Choose Library** screen. At the bottom of this screen, choose the **Create New** button.

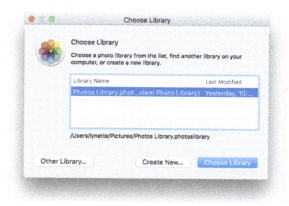

How to get your Photos out of iCloud

Name your temporary Photos Library in the **Save As** field at the top (or just leave it with the default name) and click **OK.**

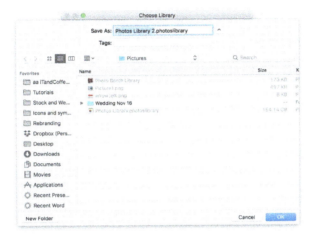

How to get the photos downloaded to this second library

You will then need to temporarily make this new library the **System Photo Library**, so that it is the main library that can interact with iCloud.

To do this, go to **Photos -> Preferences** (in the menu bar at top left).

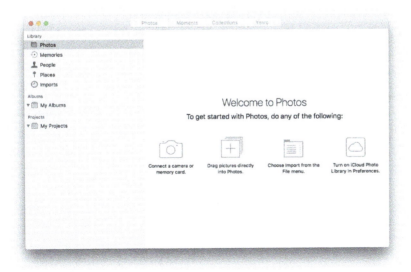

How to get your Photos out of iCloud

Click the **Use as System Photo Library** button. When you do this, the button becomes greyed to indicate this is now the System Photo Library - see below.

Then select the **iCloud** option in the same **Preferences** screen (at top of that screen).

Select/tick the **iCloud Photos Library** option and also ensure that the **Download Originals to this Mac** option is ticked.

Then sit back and wait.

How to get your Photos out of iCloud

How long will the photos download take?

The time it then takes to download your photos to your Mac will depend on
- the number of photos in your iCloud Photos Library and
- the speed of your internet.

It may take days, so you will need to be patient - and leave your device connected to the internet so the download can complete.

How do I know if the download is complete?

If the message at the bottom, of the Photos or Moments view shows something like the message here, then your download is completed.

28,589 Photos, 785 Videos
Updated Just Now

If the message instead shows that there are uploads or downloads in progress, then you will need to wait a bit longer.

When the download is completed, go back to your **Photos -> Preferences** in the temporary Photos library and turn off iCloud Photo Library.

Merge the Photos Libraries

So, the download is complete - and you now have two Photos Libraries in the Pictures folder of Finder.

These libraries now need to be merged. How is that achieved? There are a couple of options.

One is to export all the temporary library's photos into a folder on your Mac (or an external hard drive) and then import them to your original Photos Library from there. (See earlier for how to import and export.)

It is also possible to directly access the folder containing the temporary library's downloaded photos by right-clicking on the library in Pictures (from Finder) and choosing to **Show Package Contents** for the temporary photos library.

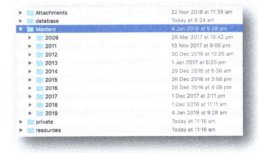

You can then import the Master folders into the original Photos library.

How to get your Photos out of iCloud

Open Original Photos Library again

Before you import the downloaded photos into the **original** photos library, you will need to re-instate it as the 'system photo library'.

To open the original Photos Library, hold the option key again as you click the Photos app. Choose the applicable file (which is usually called **Photos Library.photoslibrary**).

Go to **Photos -> Preferences** and click the **Use as system photos library** button.

If you don't intend to use iCloud Photo Library, also go to the **iCloud** option in Preferences and make sure that the **iCloud Photo Library** option is not ticked.

Import downloaded photos to Original Library

Then, go ahead with the **Import** of the folder/s of photos that you downloaded. Importing can be done in a few ways, which we described earlier in this guide.

Automatic streaming of future photos

If you want your future photos to stream from your iPhone/iPad to your Mac, make sure that **My Photo Stream** is ticked in **Photos -> Preferences -> iCloud** on the Mac.

And also make sure this same option is ticked on the iPhone/iPad.

(Note. My Photo Stream may no longer be available if your account is a new iCloud account.)

iTandCoffee guides in this series

A Guided Tour

Files, Folders and Finder

Backups, Apps and Preferences

All sorts of handy tips and features

The Photos App

For more information about iTandCoffee user guides, visit

www.itandcoffee.com.au/guides

www.ingramcontent.com/pod-product-compliance
Lightning Source LLC
Chambersburg PA
CBHW041638050326
40690CB00026B/5260